God's Promises Kept

God's Promises Kept

Devotions for Children inspired by Charles Spurgeon

Catherine Mackenzie

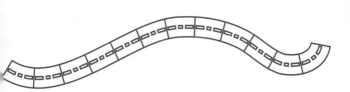

10 9 8 7 6 5 4 3 2 1

Copyright © 2021 Catherine Mackenzie
Paperback ISBN: 978-1-5271-0618-5

Published by Christian Focus Publications,
Geanies House, Fearn, Tain, Ross-shire,
IV20 1TW, Scotland, U.K.
www.christianfocus.com
email: info@christianfocus.com

Cover design by Pete Barnsley
Printed and bound in Turkey

Scripture quotations are from the King James Version
and also the author's own paraphrase.

Who was Charles Spurgeon?

Charles Haddon Spurgeon was a Baptist preacher. He was born in the United Kingdom in 1834 and by the time of his death in 1892 he was known as the "Prince of Preachers". Spurgeon was pastor of the congregation of the New Park Street Chapel and then of the Metropolitan Tabernacle in London for thirty-eight years. As well as preaching many sermons he also wrote a great many books, and hymns. Many Christians, even today, love the daily devotional book he wrote: *The Chequebook of the Bank of Faith*. This book has been based on the topics and Scriptures he used. In a culture where few use a chequebook this publication needed more than a simple rewrite. However, these little devotions have been inspired by what Spurgeon wrote. Hopefully this reimagining of some of his devotions will help a new generation to appreciate his teaching but, most importantly, the Word of God. When you see some words in the text written in red these are taken almost directly from Spurgeon's own writings. The rest are either explaining or representing what he wrote.

Catherine Mackenzie

Contents

1. Gifts and Burdens 8
2. Walking on Ice 11
3. Wiping away Tears 15
4. The Promise Keeper 20
5. Are you Afraid of the Dark? 23
6. Summer is Here! 27
7. Take Care! 31
8. Don't Play with Fire!....................35
9. Are We There Yet? 39
10. Little and Great............................43
11. Who is the Judge 47
12. Never Alone! 51
13. Freedom! 56
14. But I'm Too Young 59
15. What is a Family? 63
16. Do not be Afraid 66

17. The Poor Preacher 69

18. It's Easy to Forget 76

19. Who is Behind the Wheel? 80

20. Go to God 83

21. Are Seeds Like Jewels? 87

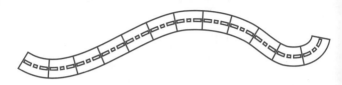

1. Gifts and Burdens

Chequebook Date: 14 January

Bible Verse: Come unto me, all ye that labour and are heavy laden, and I will give you rest (Matthew 11:28).

Some things cost money. Some things don't.

When you are given a gift it is free. It doesn't cost you anything. Your auntie doesn't wrap up your birthday gift, hand it over and then tell you to open your piggy bank. Gifts should be given with love and given freely. Nothing is freer than a gift.

God loves to give good gifts. Read the Bible verse Matthew 11:28 to find out one of the wonderful gifts God gives to those who trust in him.

When something is a gift – you don't buy it. When something is a gift – you don't borrow it. When something is a gift – you accept it, gladly.

Today's Bible verse tells us about how God gives his people rest. There are lots of things in life that make us feel tired. When the Bible says that we labour and are heavy laden – it's sin and its side effects that make us feel that way. Heavy laden is a horrible way to feel – it's like feeling tired, sad, disappointed, worried, all at the same time. When we feel like that it's because of sin.

Sin is when we want what we can't or shouldn't have. It's when we say or do things that are against God's law. It's when we think about things that are wrong and not right. When we worry about today or tomorrow that is sinful too. We should trust in the Lord Jesus Christ.

If you are worried about your sin come to Jesus and ask him to take away your sin – that is what he will do. He has promised and he always keeps his promises.

You must come to Jesus. It is important! Trust him to take care of everything.

When you come to him, the rest that he will give you will be the deepest, safest and most perfect rest ever. It will never end.

This rest will be a rest for today and for tomorrow and all your tomorrows. It will be a rest for your happiest days and your saddest. And then one day you will have a forever rest and this has a special name – Heaven.

God the Promise-keeper gives this rest to all who come to him, trusting in him for forgiveness of their sin.

What you should do: Come to Jesus, trust in him. Ask him to take away your sin.

Prayer: Thank you God, my Heavenly Father, that I can come to you for forgiveness of my sin. You have never broken a promise and never will. You never turn anyone away who seeks mercy from you. Cleanse me from my sin and make me your very own child. Amen.

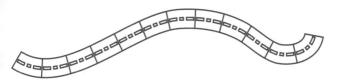

2. Walking on Ice

Chequebook Date: 24 January
Bible Verse: He will keep the feet of his saints
(1 Samuel 2:9).

Do you know what it's like to try to walk on ice or slippery mud?

It is not easy and makes it difficult for our feet to have a sure grip of the road. Sin is like slippery mud – it spoils things, can harm us and makes living a life that pleases God impossible. Sin is when we do or think or speak anything that is against God. When we do not trust in God, sin takes over our life. If we do not ask God for forgiveness, sin will cause us to be lost forever. But for those who trust God there is a rescue, a solution to the problem of sin.

God's Word promises us in 1 Samuel 2:9 that God 'will keep the feet of his saints'.

Just as a good pair of boots might stop you slipping in the mud, God will help his people from slipping and falling into sin.

Life is full of temptations that persuade us to do what is against God's law. We must trust God and obey his Word. To do this, God must help us. We can't do it on our own.

A walking stick can help us to keep steady on a muddy path. A strong friend can help us around an ice rink. God will keep us and protect us from falling into sin.

Sometimes people who go on a walk take a wrong turn. Their feet go the wrong way. Sometimes we make mistakes and foolish choices — God can protect us from that. God will stop us from wandering away from him.

Often if you go on a long walk your feet get sore. Your boots give you blisters because they don't fit properly. It makes it hard and uncomfortable to continue walking. We need God to give us strength, faith, courage and lots of other things when we are living a Christian life. God makes sure that we have everything we need to obey him. His care of us is so good that he will make us long to obey him. With his help, living for Jesus will be what we want to do most of all.

Sometimes people use nets to deliberately trap an animal. In the past, people would even use these to trap another person.

Sometimes another person will try to trap you into doing wrong. 'It's just a little white lie,' they say, or 'It's not really hurting anyone. It's only a bit of fun.' Has a friend ever said, 'Let's do this'? But you knew what they were suggesting was against God's law. All these temptations may draw you into this net of sin. But God can take you out of it.

The Bible tells us that God will make sure that we are not trapped by other people's lies or crafty plans.

With promises like this we can run without weariness and walk without fear throughout our whole lives.

What you should do: Trust in Jesus, believe in him. Obey God's Word.

Prayer: Loving Heavenly Father, I thank you that you deliver us from sin. Give me the wisdom to know when I am being tempted, and give me your strength so that I can turn away from disobedience. Thank you for the gift of your Son, Jesus Christ, the one and only saviour, who broke the power of sin and the grave. Amen.

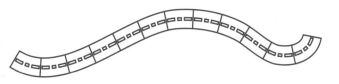

3. Wiping away Tears

Chequebook Date: 28 January
Bible verse: And God shall wipe away all tears from their eyes (Revelation 21:4).

Has someone ever wiped your face?

What are they wiping off – dirt? Smudges? Tears? Sometimes when we cry we need our tears wiped away. We're crying so much that we forget to do it. Our eyes sting, our noses run, our cheeks get red. It doesn't look pretty.

God sees and knows when his children are upset. He cares for them. He is their Heavenly Father who longs to take away their pain. God has promised in Revelation 21:4 that he 'shall wipe away all tears from their eyes'.

God promises that one day his beloved people, those who trust in his Son Jesus, will no longer be sad.

Watching the news on television can be one of the saddest things. There is hunger and disease, heartache and sorrow. But you don't have to watch the news from places far away to see sadness. It can be in our homes and streets. People say cruel words, physically hurt one another, even kill. But this sad and broken world will not be for ever. One day it will end. The sadness will be no more and there will be a new heaven and a new earth. The Bible says so.

Then there will be nothing to weep over. God himself will be with us and we will be with him – the best, closest friendship ever – with nothing to spoil it or get in the way.

There will be pleasures for ever. Tears will no longer flow. There won't even be any pain.

And those who trust in the Lord will be there in that new heaven and new earth.

Have you ever tried to imagine what heaven will be like? It is somewhere that we really look forward to – but we just can't ever imagine how truly magnificent a place it is.

Heaven will be so much better than anyone can ever imagine.

No one can wipe tears away like the God of love, but he is coming to do it.

The Bible tells us that tears may last for a night, but joy comes in the morning.

That morning, when we find ourselves with God in heaven, will be the best morning ever.

What a place to wake up in!

What you should do: Rejoice in the Lord. Be happy that God is love and that heaven is real.

Prayer: Thank you God for your promises that we know you always keep. We know that heaven is real. Your Word is always true. There isn't a single promise you have ever broken. We look forward with great excitement to being with you in heaven. Amen.

The First Promise

Genesis 3:15

I will put enmity
between you and the
woman,
And between your seed and
her Seed;
He shall bruise your head,
And you shall bruise His heel.

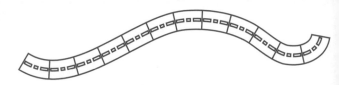

4. The Promise Keeper

Chequebook Date: 31 January
Bible verse: My God will hear me (Micah 7:7).

It's sad but sometimes the people whom we love the most hurt us.

Friends and family might quarrel with us. Angry words are said. The friend that we once thought loved us no longer wants to spend any time with us. That's when the friendship is broken. The boy or girl we used to speak with at lunchtime can't be bothered with anything we think or say.

However, God is a faithful friend and he is always listening to our requests.

When nobody else cares to listen, when we are ignored and belittled, we can turn to God.

When people are mean to you and delight to see you sad, you can turn to them and say, 'You shouldn't be so happy because I have the living God on my side. And he hears everything that I ask for.'

Because God is the living God, he can hear; because he is a loving God, he will hear; because he is our promise keeping God, he has made a binding promise that he himself will hear us.

If you can call God, 'My God', you can then say, 'My God will hear me.'

Come then and take your sadnesses to God. Tell him all about them.

Pray to him inside your heart and say, 'My God will hear me.'

You can come to Jesus and share all the problems of your heart, all the hurts, all the pain that makes you cry.

In the secret of your little room God can always hear you when you pray. Bow the knee to him because your God will hear you. Say it now: 'My God will hear me.'

What you should do: Take all your problems and cares to God. When you are sad, come to Jesus.

Prayer: Dear Heavenly Father, You can hear me so I'm taking my problems to you. My biggest problem is my sin. And you have promised forgiveness to all who trust in your Son. Thank you for listening to my requests. Forgive me in the name of Jesus. Amen.

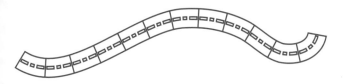

5. Are you Afraid of the Dark?

Chequebook Date: 1 February
But unto you that fear my name shall the Sun of
righteousness arise with healing in his wings
(Malachi 4:2).

Why are we sometimes afraid of the dark?

We hear something and because we can't see it, our imagination gets the better of us. Perhaps you find the dark a frustrating time because you can't do what you do through the rest of the day. When it's night-time your parents don't want you to do anything except sleep. They don't even want you to go to school.

How do you know it's night-time or morning? You look at the light. If it's early, the light will be different than night, when the sun begins to set. When it comes to evening, a time that people call dusk, the light begins to fade and the dark night draws in.

This happens every day – the sun rises and sets. In the winter the dark times might be longer and then in the summer it gets a lot lighter. The only place where it is dark throughout the whole day is somewhere called the Arctic Circle. For a while during the winter there is no sun there at all. And then during the summer the sun never sets.

But even in the Arctic Circle people know that, after the winter is over, the sun will rise again. We know when we go to bed at night the sun will appear in the morning. That's what always happens.

However, Malachi 4:2 is not talking about the sun of the morning – it's talking about the Sun of Righteousness – a person who will arise with healing in his wings. Who is the Sun of Righteousness and how does he heal us? Jesus is the Sun of Righteousness and he heals us from our sin.

Jesus is like the sun in the sky. The sun gives light to help you see. Jesus gives us spiritual light to help us see our sin, so that we will seek forgiveness from the one true God.

Jesus shines brightly with holiness. God is holy, there is nothing wrong with him at all. He is perfect.

The sun, on a warm day, makes you feel glad and cheerful. Jesus, the sun of Righteousness, gives us true joy. He is absolutely fair and faithful. He is merciful – giving us love and forgiveness when our sin deserves punishment instead.

The Bible tells us that Jesus comes with healing in his wings. Imagine you are stuck on a large cliff. There is no way off. Nobody can climb up there to help you. But just then a large eagle with strength and power comes to your rescue. Its strong wings can lift you up and take you to safety.

Jesus has more power than an eagle, and he is the only one who can heal us from our sickness of sin. He is your rescuer. You can't rescue yourself and no one else can help you – only Jesus. He is the only, true Saviour.

One day your life will end but when you trust God it will be such a glorious moment. Death may be hard but it will end with eternal life. All the days of darkness and sin will disappear and be distant, very distant memories.

When we enter God's kingdom all the sickness and sorrow of our soul will be over for ever. God has said in his Word he is perfect love, he never throws anyone away who comes to him for forgiveness. Come and bask in the warmth of God's love. He will shine forth as surely as the sun.

What you need to do: Turn away from your sin to God – this is called Repenting of your sin. Ask God to forgive you.

Prayer: Dear Lord, I thank you for the healing you promise. Thank you that sinners can come to you to be cleansed and forgiven of their sin. May I come to you today and bask in the warmth of your love. Amen.

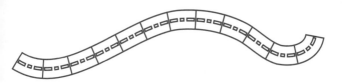

6. Summer is Here!

Chequebook Date: 2 February
Bible Verse: And ye shall go forth and grow up as calves of the stall (Malachi 4:2).

Do you notice how things change when the sun suddenly appears?

The birds start singing. The flower petals open up. People sit on deckchairs or sun loungers slapping on sunscreen and hoping for a tan.

The first days of summer usually see everyone getting out and about. Especially if it has been a long dreary winter.

Gloves and scarves are packed away and the T-shirts and swimming costumes are dragged out of the wardrobe from the year before. All of a sudden your dad will decide it's time for a barbecue and mum will let you go and buy ice creams. Everybody starts to feel happy when summer arrives.

Sometimes animals, like cattle and sheep, are kept in barns during the winter. They are delighted to get out into the sunny, green fields. The calves skip with joy when they find that they can run around and play and eat fresh grass for a change.

When you spend time with Jesus it's just like enjoying warm weather after a long winter.

Perhaps you've felt down and unhappy. Maybe you've felt despondent. Does your life sometimes feel like a damp winter days? Turning to Jesus and spending time with him can turn those bad moods into great joy – even when bad things have happened.

Spending more time with Jesus and enjoying what he has to say to us in his Word, the Bible, is like the joy that the cows feel when they get out of the stuffy barn into the fresh air.

When we come close to God in friendship, reading his Word and spending time with him in prayer, it is just a hint of what heaven is going to be like.

If it's bright and sunny outside you wouldn't decide to shut yourself away in a dark room.

If you have a Bible near at hand don't leave it sitting on the shelf – make use of it, read it, get to know God. Find out what heaven's going to be like. Enjoy God. Choosing to leave your Bible unread is as foolish as hiding inside on a glorious, sunny day.

When we look at the sheep in the field and the cows in the pasture – we see little lambs and calves there too. But they don't stay little for long, do they? Lambs and calves grow up really fast, especially if they are being fed and looked after well.

If you trust in Jesus and if you follow God, you will grow up too. You will start off as a baby Christian, but you won't always stay that way. Lambs and calves, that have a good farmer, grow up strong and grow up fast. Jesus is the one who is looking after you as a Christian – he is your Redeemer, your Saviour, the one who cares for you. He is your Good Shepherd.

When you come to know Jesus for the first time you must open your heart as a flower opens its petals to the sun. You must soak in Jesus as a sunbather soaks up the rays. Grow, grow, grow in the love and knowledge of your Lord and Saviour.

What you need to do: Don't leave God's Word on the shelf. Read it. Listen to it. Obey it. Put it inside your head and heart.

Prayer: Dear God and loving Heavenly Father, thank you that you care for me. Jesus said that his sheep shall go in and out and find pasture. May I be your lamb and feed in the rich meadows of your never-ending love. Amen.

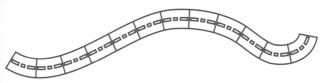

7. Take Care!

Chequebook Date: 8 February
Bible Verse: I will uphold thee with the right
hand of my righteousness (Isaiah 41:10).

Sometimes people are afraid of heights. Why is that?

It's because they are afraid of falling. Now, it's not necessary to be afraid of heights if you are just climbing up a sturdy set of steps or looking out of a window. You could say that was a bit much! However, if you're climbing up a steep cliff, or balancing on a high tree branch — then that is understandable. In fact it's even necessary. Being afraid of heights in a place like that means that you will be careful and won't take unnecessary risks. To climb somewhere that is dangerous without precautions or safety equipment is not wise.

So, if it's important to be careful in the physical world of heights and mountains, it is even more important to be careful in the spiritual world. What are the problems we face here? Well, there is the big problem of sin. Unforgiven sin is what separates us from God. It keeps us out of heaven. Sin is when we do, say, or think anything that is against God's law. Lies, unbelief, disobedience, selfish words, there is a long list of ways that we go against God. And this list is dangerous. Sin is so much more dangerous than physical injury. Unforgiven sin will send us to eternal punishment. Thankfully, there is forgiveness with our loving God. We can lean on him, trusting in him for the help and deliverance we need.

The Bible tells us that God will give us his right hand to be our help. This means that God is powerful and that he also has skill. God's right hand is a grand thing to lean upon.

You probably have a favourite hand – you're either what they call a 'Righty' or a 'Lefty'.

If you like to use your right hand then you prefer not to use your left hand. The hand that you prefer to use is the hand that you have the most strength and skill in.

God doesn't need hands, right or left, to show his power and skill. But by telling us in his Word that he will use his right hand to care for us and support us, he is telling us that not only is he strong, he is able and skilled, even dexterous. You might need to look that word up. But there is no limit to what our God can do. He will uphold us with the right hand of his righteousness. He is stretching it out to all his trusting children. We just need to grab hold of it and cling on, but we don't even have to cling on that strongly because God's grip on us is what really matters. And God's grip is the strongest.

Without God we are all in great danger, but with God we have wonderful security.

The powers of evil can do nothing to the one who is held in the hand of God.

God has promised to uphold us.

We can be bold and go forward into life and even death in that knowledge.

God always is faithful. He keeps his promises. We should be happy God will not take away his strength from us.

Even when we are at our weakest and possibly even facing death – God's eternal strength is above us, underneath us, and on either side of us. Nothing can take us out of his grasp. He is strong. We are safe. He is faithful.

What you need to do: Listen to God's warnings about sin and evil. Ask God to give you strength to fight against temptation.

Prayer: Thank you Heavenly Father, for your power and ability. I can be confident that you will do everything that you said you will do because you mean what you say. You can do anything in your power and skill. I accept the offer of your faithful, true, forgiving love. I need you now and forever. Amen.

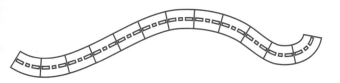

8. Don't Play with Fire!

Chequebook Date: 9 February
Bible Verse: And I will ... refine them as silver is
refined and will try them as gold is tried: they
shall call on my name and I will hear them: I will
say, It is my people: and they shall say,
The LORD is my God (Zechariah 13:9).

Have you ever been told, 'Don't play with matches!' Why is that?

It's because fire can hurt you. Fire is something that has great destructive power. A candle that is left to burn near a curtain can set that curtain alight and then the whole house could burn down. I've touched something really hot before and ended up with a big, fat blister on my thumb. That was painful, I can tell you!

But fire is also useful. Its heat, when controlled, can warm you and make food good and safe to eat.

Fire can also refine, or purify. Metals like gold and silver have to be treated with fire so that the impurities can be taken out of them. Another word for impurities is dross. When gold and silver are purified by fire they become shinier and more precious than they were before. That's why we call them precious metals. People will pay a lot for a gold ring or a piece of silver jewellery. The purer the metal, the more money is paid to purchase it.

Now, just as metals like gold and silver are precious when they have been refined, you and I are precious to God. He wants the people who trust in him to be cleaned of their dross and impurities – the sins that easily spoil our lives. How does God do that? Well, he often purifies his people by sending them trouble. The troubles and pain that believers face can be used by God to bring them closer to him. The problems and suffering of our lives can encourage us to turn away from the sins that we foolishly think are good. These hard times purify us just like a really hot fire purifies the gold metal, so that it becomes really precious.

When you are going through difficult times – when you're really struggling – you might ask God to change your life so that you don't have to experience the bad times. Sometimes, God will answer that prayer and he'll say, 'Yes, I'll do what you ask.' Sometimes he won't because he knows that your suffering is necessary – it's something that will purify you. It will actually make you ready for heaven.

God's best plan is often not to remove you from your problem, but to help you go through it. So, when God sends us struggles, we can pray that he removes them, but we can also pray as Jesus did, 'Your will be done.' We can pray that he will help us to welcome these problems rather than say, 'No, God, I don't want them.'

When God completes this process of purifying his people, we will be with him, we will be his, for ever.

What you need to do: Pray to God. Be thankful. Be content. Ask God to help you be like that.

Prayer: Father God, Help me to be thankful in all circumstances. Purify me and make me ready to be with you in heaven. Lord God you test us! This is your way and your way is the best. Help us in these difficulties that you send us and complete the process of our purifying, and we will be yours for ever and ever. Amen.

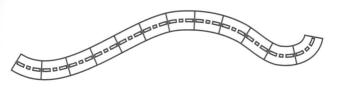

9. Are We There Yet?

Chequebook Date: 19 February
Bible Verse: Though I have afflicted thee, I will afflict thee no more (Nahum 1:12).

When I was little I hated long drives in the car.

Sometimes, before my father had been driving any distance at all, I would ask the question, 'Are we there yet?'

Have you heard the expression, 'Time drags' or 'Time moves slowly'? Time doesn't really move at different speeds as an hour is still an hour, and a day is still twenty-four hours altogether.

But sometimes it feels as though the day or night that we are going through is never going to end. When that day has pain and sorrow in it we might ask God the question, 'When is this all going to be over?'

Perhaps you wonder, 'Does God even know the answer to that question?' Well, yes he does. He is in control of everything – even pain and grief. Suffering is something that God sends and that God takes away.

If you trust in the Lord Jesus Christ, if your sins are forgiven, any suffering that you experience today will end. It might not end today or tomorrow, but there will be a day when God stops it, by taking you to be with himself in heaven.

When you are hurting, when you are worried, when you are sad – trust in the one, true, loving God. Be patient because he will answer your prayer. Everything you are going through is part of his plan.

If you can praise God in the middle of your pain, this is a great thing. You can show the world what a wonderful God he is, simply by loving him and trusting him in good times and in bad.

Have you ever enjoyed a bright sunny day, only to suddenly feel the temperature drop? A wind seems to come out of nowhere. If you are near the ocean you will see the waves rise and fall. However, just as suddenly as it appeared it will disappear. Soon you will see the seagulls floating on more gentle waves. And the waters will be calm once more. A troubled life can change just as quickly and dramatically as a troubled sea.

Sometimes it may seem that times of trouble last too long, but they will end. There will come a time in the future when we will be just as happy as we are sad right now. It is not hard for the Lord to turn night into day. He that sends the clouds can as easily clear the skies.

Be encouraged. The sad times will get better. God who allows trouble will not find it difficult to bring joy.

What you can do: Let's be excited as we wait to see the great things our God will do.

Prayer: Loving Heavenly Father, thank you that you do not find anything difficult. I have troubles, but you have power and I trust in you because you are faithful, utterly fair and endlessly loving. Amen.

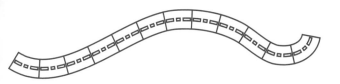

10. Little and Great

Chequebook Date: 21 February
Bible Verse: He will bless them that fear the
LORD, both small and great (Psalm 115:13).

Picture the strong athlete as he gets ready to start his race.

He is limbering up beside an old lady with a walking stick. They are going to race each other. Who do you think is going to win?

Now, imagine a large bar of chocolate on a top shelf. A little boy is trying to climb up to get it, but his big brother comes in on stilts. Who do you think will get the chocolate?

These are just two funny ways of illustrating that in life there are people who can and people who can't. Now, the people who can't are probably quite able to do something else. That granny would be great at gardening, cooking or perhaps she can use a compass?

If the bar of chocolate was hiding in a small space, right at the back of a cupboard, a little brother might find it easier than a big one to crawl in there and get the prize.

In the Bible verse we are looking at today, it tells us that God blesses all those who trust in him – both small and great.

You see, it doesn't matter to God if you are little, large, fast or slow. Perhaps nobody cares what you think or say. But God cares for you. God uses important people and unimportant people to put his plans into action. Turn to God and ask him to bless you, even if you are the tiniest person in the whole world. God can do great things with your life.

God has a great crowd of followers from across the world and history, who love and trust him. Some are little, like babies, some are great and strong, like giants. Most are simply ordinary. But all of them are blessed and to be blessed means to be truly happy.

Even if you trust in God in a very little way, you are still trusting in him and you are blessed. Even if you hope in God just a very little, you are still hoping in him and you will be forever happy.

God is the strong one. He has all the power. His love is the love that broke the power of death. Yes, you trust, yes, you hope, but it was God that gave you that trust and hope in the first place. And it is God who really holds on to you. You're in the middle of his strong grip and he's not going to let you go.

When Jesus died on the cross, did he shed more blood for the big, important people and less blood for little, insignificant people? No! The Lord Jesus bought both the small and the great with the same precious blood, and he looks after the lambs as well as the full-grown sheep.

Have you ever seen a mother look at a tiny baby and say, 'Oh that baby is too little to care for'? Not at all. A good mother spends even more love and care on a helpless baby. The smaller the baby, the more tenderly she

45

looks after it. A very tiny baby needs someone to be extra-specially gentle with it.

Now, God looks after all his people. Some think they are stronger than they are. Some don't realise how strong they are with God on their side. But the weakest Christian receives God's gentlest care. Even the strongest believer needs God's strength, forgiveness and his comfort.

People think strong, clever and fast are most important. But God protects the weak, teaches the foolish and helps the slow. God is all the strength we need.

 What you need to do: Be willing to give your life to Jesus. Look to him for strength.

Prayer: Dear loving Heavenly Father, help me to realise how much I need you. Thank you that you are the strongest. May I trust in you, love you and follow you. Amen.

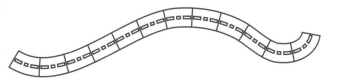

11. Who is the Judge?

Chequebook Date: 1 March
Bible Verse: Your brethren that hated you, that
cast you out for my name's sake, said, Let the
LORD be glorified: but he shall appear to your joy,
and they shall be ashamed (Isaiah 66:5).

Many people have been mistreated or even killed because they love Jesus Christ.

This is called persecution and the church across the world is greatly persecuted by those who hate Jesus. This can happen anywhere. It might happen in other countries, it can also happen in yours.

Do you know what it's like when friends make fun of you because you go to church or behave differently? That can be difficult. Those who do not trust in God hate to be reminded that they need God's forgiveness. That's when they start to bully the followers of Jesus. They do it because it's really Jesus they hate.

Throughout history, men, women and children have been hurt because they obey God. Sometimes the people who hurt them said that they were only obeying God. But they weren't. They were in fact being the enemies of God.

The verse we are looking at today says that the Lord shall appear to your joy and that the enemies of God will be ashamed. To find out how exactly that is going to happen, we need to understand that God has a job. In fact he has lots of them.

In Psalm 23, we hear about him being a shepherd. We read that, 'The Lord is my shepherd. He leads me beside still waters.'

God is also the advocate and defender of his people; and when he does so, it means a clear deliverance for those who trust in him and shame for their oppressors.

If you have ever watched a courtroom drama on T.V. you will have seen an advocate at work. The advocate is the one who stands in front of the judge to defend the prisoner. You could also call them a defence lawyer.

God defends his people when they are wrongly accused and wrongly treated. Sometimes he physically makes sure that they are released from prison, or get their job back. Sometimes that doesn't happen. But there will come a day when all wrong things are made right. On the day of judgment, all those who trust in Jesus will be given great joy and eternal life.

The enemies of God will be judged because that is another job that God has. He is the faithful and just judge of all the world.

One day, all those who hurt God's cherished children will have to answer for what they have done. God's children will be delivered from it all.

What you can do: Make a prayer diary and regularly pray for the persecuted church.

Prayer: Dear Lord, thank you that you know all that is going on. I can trust you to do everything that is right. Amen.

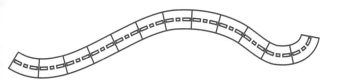

12. Never Alone!

Chequebook Date: 6 March
Bible Verse: In thee the fatherless
findeth mercy (Hosea 14:3).

Do you have a family? Who is in your family?

Do you have more people in your family group than your friends do? Perhaps you have less. I have two sisters, and lots of cousins.

Do you have friends? Do you have the same friends that you had five years ago? Do you think you'll still have the same friends in seven years that you do today? I have some friends that I've not seen in a very long time, but we're still friends.

Some people don't have mothers or fathers. Someone without parents is called an orphan.

51

Some husbands lose their wives through death. That man is called a widower.

A woman whose husband has died is called a widow.

It can be hard to lose friends and family. Sometimes they move far away, sometimes when people die it breaks our hearts.

In life we can't be certain of anything – only God. You never know when you are going to die, or when someone you love will. But we can always trust God. Even if you were to lose everything and everyone that was special to you, God is still here. You can rely on God and find in him everything that you need. It is better to have God than any other friend on the whole earth.

Even if you were totally alone, without anyone to love you, with God you are never totally alone. When God loves you and freely forgives you for your sin, you are the child of the most loving, strong, faithful Father ever. It is better to have God and no other friend than all the helpers on the earth and no God.

Have you ever been totally on your own? If you have, you might have been thankful for some peace and quiet, but sometimes you might wish for company. It's good to remember that you are never totally alone when you trust in Jesus. He is always with you. You might feel lonely, but you are never alone with God, your Heavenly Father.

One day, all those who trust in the Lord Jesus will be together with him. There will never be tears or goodbyes again.

What you can do: When you feel alone, turn to God in prayer. Look at the picture on the next page. Jeremiah, Jonah and Moses all felt alone. They all turned to God in prayer. Read: Jeremiah 17:14; Jonah 2:4; Psalm 90.

Prayer: Lord God, you have a truly loving heart towards me. Let me find mercy in you! The more needy and helpless I am, the more confidently do I appeal to thy loving heart Amen.

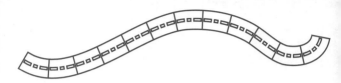

13. Freedom!

Chequebook Date: 7 March
Bible Verse: The LORD looseth the prisoners
(Psalm 146:7).

Have you ever been stuck at home and not able to go out?

Perhaps you haven't even been able to go to school, or the park, the shops or your grandparents'? That is tough. It's difficult. It's a bit like being in a prison, but not quite.

There are many Christians who have actually had to go to prison because of their faith. For many years now, in countries like Iran, Christians have been thrown in jail for believing in Jesus. Sometimes God arranges it so that these people are released from their false imprisonment.

It's amazing what God can do!

The Bible has lots of stories in it about people who were set free from prison.

Daniel obeyed God by praying three times a day. He was thrown into a lions' den as punishment. But God closed the lions' mouths.

Joseph was set free from jail and became the prime minister of Egypt. Jeremiah was thrown into a well, but Ebedmelech used some ropes and rags to pull him out. Peter was released from prison with the assistance of some angels.

There is another kind of prison though. It doesn't have iron bars, or locked doors, but it still takes away a person's freedom and liberty.

When you struggle with sadness, doubts and fears, this can be a prison to your soul. But Jesus wants to set you free. It will be a joy to Jesus to give you liberty. It will give him as great a pleasure to free you as it will be a pleasure to you to be freed.

What do you have to do to be set free? Nothing. Jesus will do it all. All you have to do is trust in him. He will be your freedom fighter. Believe in Jesus, believe that he will free you from sin with no charge or cost to you. Believe that he will free you from sin because he has all the power and is able to do it.

You can stand up and look at sin, death and the devil squarely in the face and say, 'I defy you! You loser!'

God's Word is your victory song, 'Jehovah looseth the prisoners.' Take a deep breath and shout 'FREEEEEEDOOOOM'.

What you can do: Make friends, be friendly. Write a letter to someone. Make an encouraging poster to put in your window.

Prayer: Thank you God, for the freedom you purchased for sinners through your son. Your love is great. Help us to come to you, turning away from our sin. Amen.

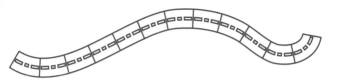

14. But I'm Too Young

Chequebook Date: 13 March
Bible Verse: Then said I, Ah, Lord GOD! behold, I cannot speak: for I am a child. But the LORD said unto me, Say not I am a child: for thou shalt go to all that I shall send thee, and whatsoever I command thee thou shalt speak (Jeremiah 1:6,7).

Do you ever feel unimportant?

Jeremiah did. He was a young man, who described himself as a child, so at the very most he would have been twelve or thirteen years of age. Jeremiah would not have known what it was like to be a ruler or even an employee. He wouldn't have had a lot of schooling or experience of the world. But God chose this young, inexperienced boy to be his special messenger.

When God sent him on an errand, Jeremiah felt rather nervous. It was a great errand and Jeremiah didn't feel up to it. He made the excuse, 'But God I'm too young for this.' God did not agree.

You see, it was God that had chosen Jeremiah to do this job. God was telling him what to say and where to go. Jeremiah didn't have to make any decisions. His words were chosen for him and he was being given all the direction and guidance he needed. God's commands just had to be followed. Jeremiah didn't have to rely on his own strength – not one bit.

Perhaps you feel nervous and anxious when a friend asks you a question about God. Maybe they want to know why you believe in Jesus, or why you don't use bad language. They see you as different and it confuses them. What do you say when they ask you questions? Do you feel unable to respond? Perhaps you feel like Jeremiah did, 'But God I'm too young. I don't know enough. It's just too difficult for little me.'

But God chooses to send Christians into the world to speak about him. He doesn't say, 'I'm going to send clever people.' He doesn't say, 'I'm only going to send people who know what they are doing.' God sends all his children. The ones who trust him and love him. So when he sends you, you must obey.

God knows how young you are, and that you have little knowledge or experience; but if he chooses to send you, it is not for you to hide away from his heavenly call.

So what if you're very young? Being very old won't make any difference. So what if you don't know that much? Even if you are the cleverest, wisest, most intelligent person ever. That won't make much of a difference either.

Old people and clever people aren't better in God's eyes than young people or those who have never passed an exam. Everyone needs forgiveness of their sins. Age and intelligence don't matter to God. God tells all his children to be his messengers, even if they have had very few birthdays.

What is the message that the children of God must bring to the world? It is a beautiful message full of hope and love. Our sins, that are many, must be forgiven and God is able and willing to do just that.

So with that message in your mind and heart, get ready to go! God has given you marching orders, so be strong and go out bravely into the world with the message of Jesus. Spread the good news in your home, on your street, throughout your school and the whole world.

What you can do: Write the good news of Jesus on the back of a postcard.

Prayer: Thank you God, that you have given your message of salvation to young and old. Help me to tell others about you even though I am nervous. Amen.

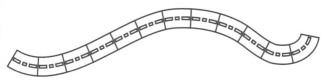

15. What is a family?

Chequebook Date: 14 March
As one whom his mother comforteth, so will I comfort you (Isaiah 66:13).

Who is in your family? Are there lots of people or just one or two?

Perhaps you have a dog or a cat? Are they members of your family? Maybe you have uncles, aunts and other friends who are considered part of your family? Who makes up a family?

Anyone who loves and trusts in the Lord Jesus Christ is part of God's forever family. The Bible tells us that those who believe in Jesus are the children of God and that God is our loving Heavenly Father. But the verse we are reading today tells us that God is not only a father, but he is also like a mother.

When a little child hurts their knee does he go and fetch the first-aid box all by himself? No, he runs to his mother. It is her love and comfort the child wants and a loving mother wants to give just that: hugs, kisses and gentle words.

The one true God, the maker of heaven and earth, wants to be like a tender, loving mother to you. Isn't that wonderful? You can come close to the Lord of heaven and be comforted by him. You can take a deep breath and be at rest in his love.

When God is your comforter, grief and heartache will not last for long.

It doesn't matter how many tears you shed, or how much you weep and cry, God will not think badly of you. When a little child sobs in her mother's arms, the mother does not turn her child away. God doesn't either.

Even if a child has hurt himself because he touched something he should not have, the mother still loves and the mother still helps. God still longs to comfort us even when we are weak, foolish and have only ourselves to blame for the state we are in. God still loves and God still helps. He is more loving and more helpful than the very best mother.

So don't try to struggle on alone. Don't think, I can do this without God. He is so loving and kind, it would be wrong to treat someone as loving as God is in this way.

Every day, start your day with God. Every day, finish your day with him. Mothers don't want to throw their children in the trash. God doesn't either. He wants to pick you up, hold you close and love you forever.

What you can do: Begin the day with our loving God, and finish it in the same company. Mothers do not get weary of loving their children and neither will God.

Prayer: Heavenly Father, thank you that you love me like a father and a mother. I don't have to go through life on my own. You are my help and strength. May I come to you for comfort, day or night. Amen.

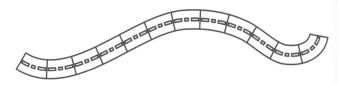

16. Do not be Afraid

Chequebook Date: 17 March
Bible Verse: Be not afraid of their faces: for I
am with thee to deliver thee, saith the Lord
(Jeremiah 1:8).

'Are you ready?' the call goes out across the battlefield.

A strong, brave captain holds his sword high. He turns to see if his army is with him, only to find that all his soldiers have run in the other direction. A great captain should be served by brave soldiers. If a captain is brave, strong and willing to fight, why should the soldiers flee?

We are in a battle. Did you know that? But we have the greatest captain ever, so we have even less reason to be afraid. God is our Captain and he is with those who are with him. God will never be away visiting or doing something else when our hour of trouble comes.

Do you have enemies – people who would threaten you? You have no need to be afraid of any man or woman who will one day die like you. They are only human. Don't be afraid.

Who is it that has ultimate power? God alone. When you don't turn to God for forgiveness and protection, you must face God's judgment alone. When you turn to God for salvation, you never have to face anything alone again. Don't be afraid when you have the all-powerful God as your protector.

Have you lost money or possessions? Perhaps a parent has lost their job, or the home you lived in now belongs to another? Trust in God, he is provides all that you need. Food, water, clothes, shelter.

Do people make fun of you? It's true that words can hurt. But we can keep going even though our bodies and our hearts are broken. Come to God. Trust in him. Jesus knows what it is like to suffer. When we suffer we experience some of the struggle he faced. But never as much as he did. The suffering we go through will, however, make us more like him in the end.

Daniel was thrown into the lions' den as punishment for his faith in the one, true God. But God brought him out of the lions' den.

Whatever trouble you face, God can make you a conqueror, a victor, a winner! The only thing you should be afraid of is being afraid.

Your worst enemy is inside you. Fear can make our souls wobble, tremble and stumble That's when we are in danger of falling into sin.

 What you can do: God is with those who are with him. God will never be away when the hour of struggle comes.

Prayer: Dear God, thank you that I can bring all my concerns to you. Help me to be as daring as Daniel with you by my side. Amen.

17. The Poor Preacher

Chequebook Date: 20 March
Bible Verse: Wherefore, if God so clothe the grass
of the field, which today is, and tomorrow is cast
into the oven, shall he not much more clothe you,
O ye of little faith (Matthew 6:30).

There once was a poor preacher, who hardly had any money to buy clothes.

In fact the suit he wore into the pulpit was threadbare and patched. In a few months' time it would be beyond the skills of his wife to repair and then what would he do? He didn't worry about it too much, however, because he was sure that God had it all under control. 'The Lord is my master and provider,' he would say to himself. 'I can trust him to find me a suit of clothes.'

Now it just so happened that one weekend a famous preacher, Charles Spurgeon, came to visit the poor preacher's congregation. Spurgeon preached and, as he read from the Scripture, it came upon his heart that he should organise a collection for the pastor. So he did. The money was gathered and the pastor found himself provided with just the right amount of money for a new set of clothes.

He had been right, all along, not to worry about his tattered suit. God had provided just what he needed.

What a wonderful story of how God provided for one poor preacher. But God provides for all his children in very similar ways. We just don't realise he is doing it.

Do you have a wardrobe full of clothes? Do you have more than one pair of shoes? Do you have clothes that keep you warm in winter and cool in summer? Do you have items that you simply wear for decoration? These may all belong to you, but God has given them.

Perhaps you are concerned about different things that you need and want. There is a difference between needs and wants. Sometimes we think we need things when in fact it is only that we want them. But our loving Heavenly Father gives us good gifts, as well as provides for our needs. However, we do not need everything we want. Whatever we receive, we are given these good things by God's hand.

Clothes are important, that's for sure. We need to be modest by wearing the right sort of clothes to cover us. Clothes are a need. But having luxurious clothes that look a certain way is not a need. So, when we need to be provided with strong boots, a warm coat, and clothes that cover us properly, we can be sure that our loving God will provide. And sometimes God is so good, he also gives us even more, by giving us some of the things we want.

Many times those who have served the Lord find that God cares for the clothes that they need to wear. God knows how important clothes are. He is the one who provided Adam and Eve with the very first clothes to cover their nakedness. Adam and Eve had sinned and when they sinned part of the punishment was a feeling of shame – shame for their sin and shame for their nakedness. God stepped in and provided clothes from them. The clothes that the Lord gave to our first parents were far better than those they made for themselves.

When we think that we can sort ourselves out, we can't. We need God to provide for us in our daily lives. We also need him to provide for our forever lives – eternity. We need salvation more than we need anything else and God is the only one who can forgive our sins.

So, when you think about your clothes think about how God provides them and all your needs. You need forgiveness more than trainers, coats or anything to wear.

God clothes the grass of the field. The lilies that grow in ponds are clothed in more splendour than kings and emperors. When God clothes plants like that, surely he will clothe his own children too. More importantly he will also clothe us with his own righteousness – a clothing so rich and perfect it is beyond price, or comparison.

God's goodness is used to cover our wickedness. No designer in the universe could come up with such a needed and perfect covering.

 What you can do: Look at your wardrobe and thank God for what is in there. Donate things that you don't need any more to charity.

Prayer: Thank you Heavenly Father, that you are our God and that you do not forget us – not even our clothes. Help us to remember that you provide all our needs and that we need you and your forgiveness most of all. Amen.

Promises from God for you

Wherefore, if God so clothe the grass of the field, which to day is, and to morrow is cast into the oven, shall he not much more clothe you, O ye of little faith? (Matthew 6:30).

Philippians 4:19
Job 38:41
Matthew 6:31-32

And the Lord shall guide thee continually, and satisfy thy soul in drought, and make fat thy bones: and thou shalt be like a watered garden, and like a spring of water, whose waters fail not (Isaiah 58:11).

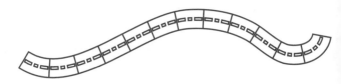

18. It's Easy to Forget

Chequebook Date: 5 April
Bible Verse: Thou art my servant: O Israel, thou shalt not be forgotten of me (Isaiah 44:21).

Have you ever forgotten something?

Sometimes I go into a room and can't remember why I went into the room in the first place. I've also set off on a journey, only to remember that I've left something important at home. It's annoying when that happens.

It's easy to forget little things – like your keys, or maybe your sports kit. There are other things that you really shouldn't forget because they are so important. Like eating, drinking or looking after someone. It would be very strange, for example, if a mum forgot to feed her baby or put him to bed.

We might be forgetful, but that's one thing that God never is. Things don't just slip his mind. His children are so precious to him, that they are always in his mind and heart.

Even if we were to fall out of his memory for just the smallest of moments, that would be a disaster for us. But it never happens. God is not absent-minded.

He does, however, choose to forget one thing and one thing only – our sin. This is not because God is careless and lets his thoughts wander. No, God chooses to forget our sin.

When our sin is covered by Christ's righteousness, then it is blotted out in much the same way that the morning mist blots out a field from our view. God's forgetting is a deliberate act on his part – not a mistake.

However, throughout everything that happens, he never forgets you – his child. You might be forgotten by a parent or a friend. Someone might change from being a friend to an enemy. But God will never change and he will never forget any of his true servants.

God ties himself to us not by what we do for him, but by what he has done for us. We have been loved too long, and bought at too great a price to be forgotten. Jesus never can forget.

When God is close by you, never to be separated, it is not because you are holding on to him but because he is holding on to you.

When Jesus sees you, he sees the pain he went through to save you.

When God sees you, he sees how precious you are to his Son.

When the Holy Spirit sees you, he sees you as the great, successful work of salvation that you are.

You will never be overlooked. You are always in God's thoughts. You will be constantly strengthened because God does not forget.

What you can do: God does not forget you. Do not forget God.

Prayer: God and loving Heavenly Father, help me to remember you and your Word. May I never forget how much you have given up for me, how much you love me, how strong and forgiving you are. Amen.

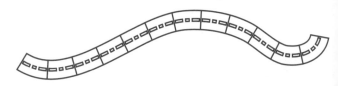

19. Who is Behind the Wheel?

Chequebook Date: 14 April
Bible Verse: He shall choose our inheritance for us
(Psalm 47:4)

Have you ever been in a boat?

I have been in several. Once I drove one. It belonged to my uncle. However, for some reason I could only get the boat to go in circles and soon everyone on board was feeling rather seasick. My uncle thankfully took the wheel out of my hand and everybody breathed a sigh of relief.

I had very little idea of what I was doing. Leaving the boat under my direction would have been foolish and dangerous. We could have ended up anywhere – possibly even at the bottom of the ocean, rather than floating on the top.

Sometimes we like to think that we are in charge of our lives. We want to make the decisions. But a wiser mind than ours arranges our destiny or future. God makes the rules. And we should be glad of this. God makes good choices, the best choices, so we should be happy to choose God, so that he makes these choices for us. If you trust in God, then the best thing that you can have is for all things to go God's way.

We are a lot safer when we let God take the wheel – when we let him make the good choices for our lives.

If things are going wrong in our lives – we can leave the painful present with God.

If things have been difficult growing up – we can leave our heartbreaking histories with God.

If things are uncertain and scary and we don't know what's to come – we can leave our fearful futures with God.

He is our heavenly father, our constant comforter and our Saviour.

A wiser mind than our own arranges our destiny. The ordering and deciding of all things is with God. This makes us glad. What should our choice be? We choose that God should choose for us. He should make our choices and decisions.

What you can do: If some people say God is not in charge – I'm the boss – tell them that you are as free as you could ever be when you let God take control.

Prayer: Lord, may I not be foolish, but wise, by letting you guide me and direct me. Please take control. I want you to be the driver of my life. Amen.

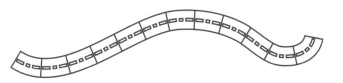

20. Go to God

Chequebook Date: 30 March
Bible Verse: Be careful for nothing; but in
everything by prayer and supplication with
thanksgiving let your requests be made known
unto God. And the peace of God, which passeth
all understanding, shall keep your hearts and
minds through Christ Jesus (Philippians 4:6,7).

Sometimes it might be hard to trust someone.

For example, if you were standing on top of a wall and a friend said, 'Jump, I'll catch you.' You might wonder if they are able to do it? However, if you are in a swimming pool and your big brother says, 'Jump in and I'll catch you' – that might be different? Why? You know if your brother is strong enough to hold on to you in the water. You know him!

Then, if you were in your house and wanted to have a seat, you would just walk over to a chair and sit down, wouldn't you? You know the chair, you've used it before, you trust that it will bear your weight. That's what chairs are designed to do.

Trusting that God will do what he says he will do, is the same as sitting on a chair. It's a simple act of trust on your part. But your trust doesn't make the chair strong. The chair is as strong as it is.

God is all-powerful. Your trust doesn't make God any stronger, but to really enjoy his strength you have to trust.

Go to God with your cares – go to him in prayer. Instead of anxiety, you will have a wonderful conversation with God.

Sometimes we have longings, things that we really want. God provides our needs, but he understands our longings too. He knows that there are other things that we want to have. We may not really need these things, but we still want them. God knows our hearts. Carry these desires to the Lord of your life, the guardian of your soul. He knows what is good for you and what isn't. Trust him in all things, be content to accept what he gives you and to be thankful when he doesn't give you everything you ask for.

When you bring these desires to your loving Heavenly Father, don't forget to thank him for all that he is and all that he does. Be thankful for him, not just for what he gives you. And don't doubt him – enjoy him for the loving, faithful, powerful Father God that he is.

Hide nothing from your loving Heavenly Father. If there is even the smallest little want buried away inside your heart, you should bring it to him. The Bible says that we are to 'make known our requests' to God. He gives wonderful things to his beloved children. He may give your request now, or later, or not all. Remember he does know best. You, as his child, should always feel free to bring any concern or want to God. No matter what the outcome is in the end, telling God how you feel is never a bad thing.

Bringing our problems to God is the best place for them. When you trust in Jesus, your sins are covered by Jesus. You can come to God with complete confidence. And what peace that will bring you!

If you have ever had a great big bear hug from someone you haven't seen in a long time – that is like God's peace. In fact, God's peace is even better – it's a never-ending bear hug. Your heart and mind will be completely at rest. No matter what happens in your life, even if you face death, poverty, pain, gossip, you shall live in Jesus. No storm will throw you off track, you will rise above every dark cloud.

What you should do: Do not pray doubtfully, but thankfully. Hide nothing from God. 'Make known your requests.' Go only to your God, the Father of Jesus, who loves you in him.

Prayer: Dear Lord and Heavenly Father, I believe your Word, but I need your help to do this. Please stop me from doubting you. Amen.

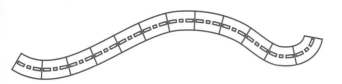

21. Are Seeds Like Jewels?

Chequebook Date: 2 May
Bible Verse: He that soweth to the Spirit shall of
the Spirit reap life everlasting (Galatians 6:8).

You don't throw jewels away!

If you saw someone throwing diamonds down at his feet as he walked through a field you would wonder, 'What is that guy up to? He'll never find those again.' What use are expensive jewels when they are thrown into the dirt?

So, when a farmer throws seed into the soil is he wasting that seed? Is he throwing it away never to be seen again? No, because seeds are different from jewels. Seeds are amazing and much more useful. Seeds have life in them. That's why when you bury a seed in the soil it isn't a waste. The seed sprouts and grows and you get even more seeds in the end!

When you sow seeds you are not throwing things away to be lost and destroyed, you are burying them in the ground so that they will bring life and fruit when the right season comes. Sowing seeds in the right soil brings life.

God's Word is like seed, and when it comes into a person's heart and mind it can bring great life – spiritual life. What is spiritual life? It is trusting and loving God and obeying his commands.

If you study (or sow) God's Word into your life you will learn to love him and glorify him. This is called 'sowing to the Spirit'. Sowing God's Word in your life brings strength and power to your soul, the part of you that loves God or decides to love something else instead.

A wheat seed grows wheat, which we make into bread. An apple seed grows apples, which we can eat for a snack or put into a pie. A potato planted in the ground gives you more potatoes, ones you can boil, or mash, or make into chips or fries. A farmer is pleased to see a healthy crop of vegetables. God is delighted when his children honour him. If you trust in God and obey him, your life is like a glorious fruit that pleases the Lord. God's Word gives you God's strength to live a life that pleases God. You are brought closer to God and you will long to spend more time with him.

When farmers work in a field sometimes their harvests are good, but sometimes they fail. Sometimes things in our lives go well and sometimes they don't. We often put a lot of energy into making money or getting the latest fashions. But these things never last. Like a bad harvest they fail us. However, the life and fruit that God gives lasts forever. Honour God. Obey him. This is what is most important – more important than money or harvests.

Farmers sometimes have a party when the crops are gathered. Everyone is happy and enjoys the chance to relax after a summer of very hard work. The crops are stored in the barn for the winter ahead and the farmer can take a rest. If you trust in Jesus, at the end of your life there will be a great festival party in heaven. We will thank God for what he has done and God will welcome his children home with a big 'Well done.'

What you can do: This life flows on like an ever-deepening, ever-widening river, till it brings us to the ocean of unending peace where the life of God is ours for ever and ever. Study God and live for him so that life shall be our reward, even everlasting life.

Prayer: Dear Lord and loving Heavenly father, help us to work for you and not for ourselves. As we study and obey your Word give us a longing for heaven, to be with you, Amen.

Deuteronomy 12:28

Observe and obey all these words which I command you, that it may go well with you and your children after you forever, when you do what is good and right in the sight of the Lord your God.

Charles Spurgeon
Who Is the Greatest?
Catherine MacKenzie

Charles Spurgeon preached from the Bible in a way that
ordinary people could understand. He even acted out Bible
passages and would pace back and forth dramatically! He
was a great preacher, but he knew that it was God who was
behind this. It was God who made Spurgeon great.

ISBN: 978-1-5271-0393-1

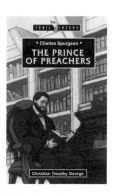

Charles Spurgeon
Prince of Preachers
Christian George

Charles Spurgeon was a simple country lad who went on to become one of the best known preachers in London, Europe and the world. Caught in a snowstorm one day when he was a teenager, he crept into the back of a church and the words, "Look unto Jesus and be saved!" changed his whole life. Charles spoke words that touched the hearts of rich and poor alike. His fame became so widespread that it is reputed that even Queen Victoria went to hear one of his sermons. Charles was more concerned about the King of Kings - Jesus Christ.

ISBN: 978-1-78191-528-8

Fascinating Bible Facts Vol. 1
103 Devotions
Irene Howat

- A fact–finding expedition through the Bible
- Small, exciting devotionals for 7 – 12 year olds
- Padded hardback giftbook with Ribbon

There are some surprising stories in God's Word about animals, trees and forests, and families – amongst other things. In this book you will find out about the beginning of time, but also discover the most amazing place that ever was or will be – heaven!

ISBN: 978-1-5271-0143-2

Fascinating Bible Facts Vol. 2
104 Devotions
Irene Howat

- A fact–finding expedition through the Bible
- Small, exciting devotionals for 7 – 12 year olds
- Padded hardback giftbook with Ribbon

Discover the names of Jesus and what the word 'Bible' means while following the life of Jesus from his birth through to his death and resurrection.

ISBN: 978-1-5271-0144-9

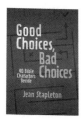

Good Choices, Bad Choices
Bible Characters Decide
Jean Stapleton

- 44 devotional readings with Scripture references
- Decisions made by Bible characters
- Includes 'Thinking Further' questions

From the first wrong choice made by Adam and Eve, throughout the Bible we meet many people who chose well or who made foolish decisions.

ISBN: 978-1-5271-0527-0

More Good Choices, Bad Choices
Bible Characters Decide
Jean Stapleton

- 44 devotional readings with Scripture references
- Learn about wise and foolish choices
- Includes 'Thinking Further' questions

Young and old, rich and poor all appear in the Bible and through them we see examples of people who made wise and foolish decisions.

ISBN: 978-1-5271-0528-7

CHRISTIAN FOCUS PUBLICATIONS

Christian Christian CF4K Mentor
Focus Heritage

Christian Focus Publications publishes books for adults and children under its four main imprints: Christian Focus, CF4K, Mentor and Christian Heritage. Our books reflect our conviction that God's Word is reliable and Jesus is the way to know him, and live for ever with him.

Our children's publication list includes a Sunday School curriculum that covers pre-school to early teens, and puzzle and activity books. We also publish personal and family devotional titles, biographies and inspirational stories that children will love.

If you are looking for quality Bible teaching for children then we have an excellent range of Bible stories and age specific theological books.

From pre-school board books to teenage apologetics, we have it covered!

Find us at our web page:
www.christianfocus.com

CF4•K
Because you're never
too young to know Jesus